DEMOCRACY

The Evolution, Challenges, and Future of Government by the People

Patrick Odega

ISBN: 9798393395728

Dedication

To all the men and women throughout history who have fought, sacrificed, and even died for the principles of democracy - political equality, individual rights, and government by the people. Your courage and conviction have inspired generations to come, and your legacy serves as a reminder of the enduring importance of these values. This book is dedicated to you and your unwavering commitment to the cause of freedom and justice for all.

May your efforts continue to inspire and guide us as we strive to build a more equitable, inclusive, and democratic world. Your legacy reminds us that democracy is not just a political system, but a way of life - one that requires constant vigilance, participation, and renewal. Let us honor your memory by working tirelessly to defend and strengthen democracy, so that it may continue to be a beacon of hope and opportunity for all people, in all places, for generations to come.

Table of Contents

Chapter 1:
Introduction

Democracy is a system of government in which power is held by the people, either directly or through elected representatives. It is a form of government that has been embraced by many nations around the world, and is considered by many to be the most just and equitable way of governing a society.

A. Definition of Democracy:

At its core, democracy is based on the principles of popular sovereignty, political equality, and majority rule. In a democratic system, the people have the power to choose their leaders and to participate in the decision-making process. This can be done either through direct democracy, where citizens vote on laws and policies directly, or through representative democracy, where citizens elect officials to represent them in the decision-making process.

B. Historical Background of Democracy:

The concept of democracy dates back to ancient Greece, where the city-state of Athens practiced a form of direct democracy in which citizens participated in the government directly. However, it was not until the Enlightenment era of the 18th century that the modern concept of democracy began to take shape. The American and French Revolutions of the late 18th century established the idea of popular sovereignty and political equality, and the concept of democracy continued to evolve in the 19th and 20th centuries as more nations embraced the idea of government by the people. Today, democracy is widely considered to be a fundamental principle of modern governance, and a cornerstone of human rights and social justice.

Chapter 2:
Types of Democracy

A. Direct Democracy:

Direct democracy is a form of government in which citizens participate directly in the decision-making process. In this system, citizens vote on laws and policies directly, rather than electing representatives to do so on their behalf. Direct democracy is often associated with small communities or groups, and is less common in larger societies due to logistical challenges.

B. Representative Democracy:

Representative democracy is a form of government in which citizens elect representatives to make decisions on their behalf. In this system, citizens have the power to vote for representatives who they believe will best represent their interests and make decisions on their behalf. Representative democracy is the most common form of democracy in the world today.

C. Presidential Democracy:

Presidential democracy is a form of representative democracy in which a president serves as both the head of state and the head of government. In this system, the president is elected directly by the people and has significant power to make decisions and set policies.

D. Parliamentary Democracy:

Parliamentary democracy is a form of representative democracy in which the government is formed by the party or coalition of parties that has the support of the majority in parliament. In this system, the prime minister serves as the head of government, and the monarch or president serves as the head of state. Parliamentary democracy gives citizens a direct voice in the decision-making process through their elected representatives in parliament.

Chapter 3: Democratic Institutions

A. Executive Branch:

The executive branch is responsible for enforcing the laws and policies of a government. In a democratic system, the executive branch is headed by an elected official, such as a president or prime minister, who is responsible for making decisions and setting policy. The executive branch also includes a number of agencies and departments that are responsible for carrying out the day-to-day operations of the government.

B. Legislative Branch:

The legislative branch is responsible for making the laws of a government. In a democratic system, the legislative branch is typically made up of elected representatives, who are responsible for drafting and passing laws. The legislative branch is also responsible for overseeing the actions of the executive branch, and has the power to impeach officials who are deemed to have acted improperly.

C. Judicial Branch:

The judicial branch is responsible for interpreting the laws and ensuring that they are applied fairly and consistently. In a democratic system, the judicial branch is typically made up of judges who are appointed or elected to their positions. The judicial branch has the power to interpret the constitutionality of laws and policies, and to enforce the rights of citizens and other legal entities.

D. Electoral Systems:

Electoral systems are the mechanisms by which citizens choose their representatives in a democratic system. There are many different types of electoral systems, including first-past-the-post, proportional representation, and ranked-choice voting. The choice of electoral system can have a significant impact on the outcome of elections and the representation of various groups within a society.

E. Political Parties:

Political parties are organizations that seek to gain political power by running candidates for elected office. In a democratic system, political parties serve as a means for citizens to organize and advocate for their preferred policies and candidates. Political parties can have a significant impact on the functioning of democratic institutions, and can influence the policy decisions of elected officials.

Chapter 4: Democratic Values

At the heart of democratic institutions are a set of values that promote freedom, equality, and justice for all citizens. These values form the foundation of democratic societies and guide the actions of individuals and institutions within these societies. Some of the key democratic values include:

A. Equality:

Equality is a fundamental democratic value that promotes the idea that all individuals should have equal rights and opportunities, regardless of their race, gender, religion, or other characteristics. Equality is enshrined in many democratic constitutions and is a cornerstone of democratic institutions.

B. Liberty:

Liberty is another important democratic value that promotes the idea that individuals should have the freedom to pursue their own interests and goals without undue interference from the government or other institutions. Liberty is often associated with individual rights such as freedom of speech, freedom of assembly, and freedom of religion.

C. Justice:

Justice is a value that promotes fairness and equality in the distribution of resources and opportunities. In a democratic system, justice is often achieved through a system of laws and regulations that are designed to protect the rights and interests of all citizens, and to ensure that those who violate these rights are held accountable.

D. Tolerance:

Tolerance is a value that promotes the idea that individuals and groups should be respected and valued for their differences, rather than discriminated against or persecuted. Tolerance is essential to the functioning of democratic institutions, as it allows individuals and groups with different perspectives and interests to work together to achieve common goals.

E. Pluralism:

Pluralism is a value that recognizes the diversity of opinions, beliefs, and perspectives within a society, and promotes the idea that all voices should be heard and considered in the decision-making process. Pluralism is essential to the functioning of democratic institutions, as it ensures that all citizens have a voice in the policies and decisions that affect their lives.

Democratic values are essential to the functioning of democratic institutions, and provide a framework for promoting freedom, equality, and justice for all citizens. By upholding these values and working to ensure that they are enshrined in laws and institutions, we can continue to build more inclusive, equitable, and democratic societies that serve the needs and aspirations of all people.

Chapter 5: Challenges to Democracy

While democratic institutions are designed to ensure that citizens have a voice in the decision-making process, there are a number of challenges that can threaten the integrity and effectiveness of these institutions. Some of the key challenges to democracy include:

A. Corruption:

Corruption is a major challenge to democratic institutions, as it can erode public trust in the government and lead to a concentration of power in the hands of a few individuals or groups. Corruption can take many forms, including bribery, embezzlement, and abuse of power.

B. Voter Suppression:

Voter suppression refers to efforts to prevent certain groups of people from exercising their right to vote, often through tactics such as gerrymandering, voter ID laws, and restrictive voting policies. Voter suppression can undermine the legitimacy of democratic institutions and reduce the diversity of voices and perspectives represented in government.

C. Polarization:

Polarization refers to the growing divide between different groups within a society, often along political or ideological lines. Polarization can make it more difficult for elected officials to work together and compromise on policy decisions, and can lead to a breakdown in democratic institutions and processes.

D. Disinformation:

Disinformation refers to the spread of false or misleading information with the intent of manipulating public opinion. Disinformation can undermine the credibility of democratic institutions and reduce public trust in the government, and can be particularly damaging in the context of elections and other political processes.

Despite the many challenges facing democratic institutions, democracy remains one of the most effective and inclusive forms of government yet devised. By working together to address the challenges facing our democratic systems, we can ensure that these institutions continue to serve the needs and aspirations of citizens around the world, both now and in the future.

Chapter 6: Democratic Transitions

Democratic transitions refer to the process by which a society moves from an authoritarian or undemocratic system of government to a democratic one. This process can be long and difficult, and is often marked by challenges and setbacks. Some key aspects of democratic transitions include:

A. Case Studies of Successful Transitions:

There have been many successful democratic transitions throughout history, including the transition from apartheid in South Africa to a democratic government, and the transition from military rule in Brazil to a civilian government. By studying these successful transitions, we can learn valuable lessons about the factors that contribute to their success, such as strong civil society movements, effective leadership, and international support.

B. Lessons from Failed Transitions:

There have also been many failed democratic transitions, such as the transition to democracy in Iraq following the 2003 US-led invasion. By examining these failed transitions, we can learn important lessons about the factors that contribute to their failure, such as weak institutions, lack of leadership, and inadequate support from the international community.

C. International Support for Democracy:

International support for democracy is a critical factor in successful democratic transitions. This support can take many forms, including financial assistance, technical assistance, and diplomatic support. By providing this support, the international community can help to build strong democratic institutions, promote respect for human rights, and create a culture of democracy that can help to sustain democratic transitions over the long term.

Democratic transitions are an important process through which societies can move from authoritarianism to democracy, and can be challenging and complex. By studying successful and failed transitions, and by providing support for democratic institutions, we can help to promote the growth and sustainability of democracy around the world.

Chapter 7: The Future of Democracy

The future of democracy is an important topic of discussion, as societies around the world continue to face new challenges and opportunities. Some key aspects of the future of democracy include:

A. Technological Advancements and Democracy:

Technological advancements are transforming the way we live and work, and are also having a significant impact on democracy. From the rise of social media and fake news, to concerns about privacy and surveillance, technology is changing the way we engage with democracy. It is important for democratic institutions to adapt to these changes, and to ensure that they are equipped to respond to the challenges and opportunities that arise from technological advancements.

B. Climate Change and Democracy:

Climate change is one of the most pressing issues facing the world today, and is also having a significant impact on democracy. As communities around the world are affected by the impacts of climate change, it is important for democratic institutions to respond to these challenges and to ensure that the voices of affected communities are heard.

C. Globalization and Democracy:

Globalization is another important factor that is shaping the future of democracy. As economies become more interconnected and the world becomes more integrated, it is important for democratic institutions to adapt to these changes and to ensure that they are able to respond to the needs of their citizens in a globalized world.

D. Education and Democracy:

Education is a critical factor in the future of democracy, as it plays a key role in promoting informed and engaged citizenship. By investing in education and promoting access to information, democratic institutions can help to build a more informed and engaged citizenry that is able to participate meaningfully in the democratic process.

The future of democracy is shaped by a variety of factors, including technological advancements, climate change, globalization, and education. By understanding and responding to these challenges and opportunities, democratic institutions can help to build a more inclusive, equitable, and sustainable democratic future for all citizens.

Conclusion

In conclusion, democracy is a complex and multifaceted system of government that is characterized by a commitment to the values of equality, liberty, justice, tolerance, and pluralism. From its historical origins to its modern-day manifestations, democracy has played a critical role in shaping the course of human history, and remains an important topic of discussion and debate around the world.

A. Summary of Key Points:

Throughout this discussion, we have explored the definition and historical background of democracy, the various types of democracy, the key democratic institutions, values, and transitions, and the future of democracy in a rapidly changing world. By examining these different aspects of democracy, we have gained a deeper understanding of the challenges and opportunities that democracy faces, and the ways in which democratic institutions can adapt and evolve to meet these challenges.

B. Reflections on the Importance of Democracy:

Reflecting on the importance of democracy, we can see that it plays a critical role in promoting human rights, political stability, and economic development. By providing citizens with a voice in their own governance, democracy helps to build a more inclusive and equitable society, where the needs and concerns of all citizens are taken into account. Furthermore, by promoting transparency, accountability, and the rule of law, democracy helps to prevent corruption and ensure that power is wielded responsibly.

C. Recommendations for Strengthening Democracy:

To strengthen democracy in the years ahead, it is important to continue investing in democratic institutions, promoting access to information and education, and supporting civil society organizations that work to promote democracy and human rights. Furthermore, it is important to recognize and address the various challenges and threats facing democracy today, such as technological advancements, climate change, and globalization. By working together to address these challenges, and by promoting the values and institutions of democracy, we can help to build a more sustainable and inclusive democratic future for all citizens.